SALTY W
Pat Ingo

Pat Ingoldsby has written two highly successful plays for children — *Rhymin' Simon* and *Yeukface the Yeuk and the Spotty Grousler*. Both plays have been presented by the National Theatre as their 'Christmas at the Peacock' season in 1979 and 1982.

Two of Pat's plays for adults — *Hisself* and *When am I Gettin' Me Clothes?* have played to packed houses at the Peacock Theatre. A further play enjoyed similar success at the Gaeity Theatre.

Five of Pat's radio plays have been broadcast by RTE Radio One ... *The Dark Days of Denny Lacey, She Came Up From the Sea, Fire Is Far Enough, Liffey Ever Is* and a radio adaptation of *When Am I gettin' Me Clothes?*

Pat is firmly established as the children's favourite figure on television thanks to the phenomenal success of his 'Pat's Hat' and 'Pat's Chat' shows. His stories for children have built up a huge following in the *Irish Press* and they regularly delight young viewers of 'Bosco'. His book *Zany Tales* was a bestseller.

Four collections of Pat's poetry have been published to date — *You've Just Finished Reading This Title, Rhyme Doesn't With Reason, Up the Leg of Your Jacket* and *Welcome To My Head*. He is a regular performer at arts festivals, on the university circuit and in children's venues. He writes a weekly humourous column in the *Evening Press* and contributes poems to *In Dublin*. His hosting of the chat show 'Saturday Live' and unforgettable appearance on 'The Late Late Show' re-enforced his unique position as one of this country's most mercurial characters.

THE O'BRIEN PRESS

PAT INGOLDSBY

SALTY WATER

THE O'BRIEN PRESS
DUBLIN

First published 1988 by The O'Brien Press Ltd.
20 Victoria Road, Rathgar, Dublin 6, Ireland

British Library Cataloguing in Publication Data
Ingoldsby, Pat
Salty water.
I. Title
821.914

ISBN 0-86278-178-8

Typeset in Palatino at The O'Brien Press.
Book design: Michael O'Brien.
Cover design: The Graphiconies
Printed by: The Guernsey Press Co. Ltd.,
Guernsey, Channel Islands

If you are reading these words right now,
this book is specially for you.

If any of these poems ever surface in school or college
textbooks when I'm dead and gone, I'll come back and
haunt whoever's responsible.

Contents

Up and Down the Strip

It's the tingle between your legs
that takes you down to Leeson Street,
down to The Strip
down to meet
tight jeans tight thighs
denim bottoms hopes high
standing and sitting
sipping the wine
buy you a bottle
make you mine
and the Stones
can't get no satisfaction.

Business men working late
grey haired overweight
white shirts club ties
credit cards white lies
cigar smoke bald spots
big stomachs big shots
wrinkles over rugby scars
randy thoughts company cars
and the Stones
can't get no satisfaction.

Eyes meet look away
how do you start?
what do you say?
look unmarried
like you couldn't care less
look unfrustrated

they'll never guess
pray to God that
your daughter's not here
hold in your stomach
swallow your fear
grab two glasses
bottle of wine
take a sip
make you mine
and the Stones
can't get no
satisfaction.

Jump suits open zipped
legs crossed leather hipped
tight jeans young blood
long skirts looking good
some do some don't
how can you tell
which one won't
more important
which one will
onto the dance floor
get in for the kill
dance fast dance slow
move in closer
now you know
dance fast dance slow
nuzzle the neck
here we go
will you take off
your clothes?

No! Not down here!
and not in my place
no bloody fear
you'll waken the wife
disturb the kids
we'll do it in your place
keep it all hid
and the Stones
can't get no satisfaction.

Up the steps
tired and slow
she drank your wine
she's still below
up the steps
tired and slow
the taxis are waiting
all in a row
and the Stones
can't get no satisfaction.

No Weirdos Please

Sitting alone in Bewleys.
The guy at the next table
couldn't keep his eyes off me.
'Psssst,' he said
'Are you Native-Speaking
            Bi-Sexual
            Box-Number 873
who seeks help in improvising
the Kama Sutra through
the medium of Irish
No weirdos need apply?'

I shook my head.

'Not I ... I'm middle-aged hippy
who has never had it
at 16,000 feet because
I'm scared stiff of flying
Photo appreciated.'

'Pssst,' said the girl
behind the newspaper.
'Are you Rough Raw Randy
but very sincere Psychopath
who seeks lasting relationship
until tomorrow morning with
perverted dental receptionist
who plays the accordion
the imaginative way?'

I shook my head.

'Not today
but I'm willing to learn.'

I was secretly waiting to meet
long leggy lepidopterist
wild willing but discreet
who is into assertion training
for insects
seeks man with own supply
of spiders
and fifteen-foot extension flex.

She never did show
and so
I'm sitting alone in Bewleys
trying hard not to look
like a Box-Number.

An Awful Lot of Salty Water

Twenty-seven years
of unshed tears
is an awful lot
of salty water
locked in
blocked up
damned
behind his eyes.
Holy God
if that man ever cries
he'll surely drown somebody.

Twenty-seven years
of blocking the flood
denying the flow
smiling so that
no one will
No! No! Go away
come again some other day
everybody's looking
I don't want them to see
No! No!
Let me be
Let me be
a man.

A childhood ago
he fell
he fell
and cut his knee
Come on now little man

mustn't let your sister see
blow your nose
wipe your eyes
Mammy's soldier
never cries.

Same again
when granny died
mother trembled
sister cried
father stiffened
upper lip
Mammy's soldier
choked inside
blow your nose
wipe your eyes
Mammy's soldier
never cries.

Block the flow
dam the flood
crying never did no good
spilt milk
dead and gone
playground sissies
are trampled on
toughen up
learn the plan
put in the boot
be a man
hold it back
hold it brave

you're building up
a tidal wave
dam it
deny it
any way you can
dam it
deny it
be a man.

Listen …
hear the whisper
gentle, slow
let it happen
let it go
salty trickle
salty flow
wash your cheeks
wash and grow
feel it building
feel the flood
salty torrent
it's yours
it's good
tears
as much a part of you
as anything else
your body can do
Mammy's soldier
is bursting the dam
Mammy's soldier
is becoming a
man …

Put the Cork in Tight

I wrote a message in a bottle
and threw it into the sea.
It was a very simple message.
'I am on this beach right now
and would like to meet you
whoever and wherever you are.
I am alone.'
I got an answer six months later.

'Which fucking beach is it?'

Lovingly I wrote a reply.

'Who the hell do you think you are?
That's no way to answer a message in a bottle.
eh ... P.S. Dollymount Strand.'

I got a reply nine months later.

'Listen shithead - I've read your last message
and now I'm pregnant.
You mustn't have corked the bottle properly
Solicitor's letter to follow in next bottle.'

I wrote across the label - 'Gone away -
Not known at this beach.'
Then I hitched to Galway
and threw it into the Atlantic.
Thanks be to God for the Gulf Stream.

Do You Know This Girl?

Her best friend used to go out
with Bono's second cousin.
She knows somebody
who knows somebody in RTE
so she danced on Megamix.
She has been photographed
at The Boat Show
   The Horse Show
   The Spring Show
   every other show
where you get your picture
in the paper if you wear
sunglasses on top of your head
and your address is not
Finglas, Ballyfermot or Tallaght.
She talks to people from
Finglas, Ballyfermot or Tallaght
only if they play in a rock band
and are tipped in the right polls
as 'The New Band most likely to succeed.'
She buys expensive jeans in expensive shops
and cuts the bollix out of them with a scissors.
She was very nearly mentioned in 'An Irishman's Diary'
but they mentioned Seamus Heaney instead.
Her other best friend knows a girl
who used to live next door to The Edge.
She went to T.C.D.
until she discovered that
none of her best friends
knows anybody who corrects

the exam papers
and you don't automatically
get free tickets for the Trinity Ball.
Small children frighten her.
If she ever has any of her own
they will appear on the cover
of whichever glossy magazine
happens to be 'In' at the time
because her husband will know
somebody who knows the photographer.
If you speak with a Dublin accent
she will expect you to be
a builder's labourer/unemployed/
an unemployed builder's labourer
unless you happen to be Brush Shiels
in which case she'll expect to get
on the front of your next album.
Her second-best friend met Bob Geldof
backstage at Self-Aid.
She was there too because she knew
somebody who knew somebody in RTE.
U2 would have personally presented her
with a signed copy of The Joshua Tree
if only somebody had told them about
her many connections with the band.
She got a couple of pounds off it anyway
because Daddy knows Richard Branson's
aircraft mechanic.
Apart from being a good subject for a poem
she doesn't interest me in the slightest
and I very much doubt
whether she'd be even

vaguely interested in me.
I don't know anyone who
ever lived next door to
anybody.

So Well You Might.

My father and mother
used to sleep in this bed
but now he is dead and buried.
My mother sleeps alone
in the room next door
where me and my brothers
used to laugh and joke and snore.
I lie awake
in my parent's old double bed.
My father's dog
is cradling his head
against me
and is sighing in the night.
So well you might, Tandy,
So well you might ...

Gay, Me Arse

Down the bright white steps
into the twilight club
where nighttime hunters hunt
and flit and sit in black shadow corners
and there are no women
only black mascara eyes
with long dark lashes
and there are no women
only black tights clinging tight
and fingers tipping touch
and tongues touching tip
and there are no women
only men who play
the active and the passive.
Some are wearing skirts
and some are not,
Some are finger touching
and some are finger touched
some are sitting in the corners
hoping to be found
and some are flitting into corners
and flitting all around
and there's an ebb and there's a flow.

Up there in the outside street,
the men are pressing women
into late dark doorways
and hungry mouthing lips,
Up there the men are pressing women
into doorways and jagged teething zips

But that's alright baby that's alright.
Down here the men are looking for the boys
and the boys are searching for the men
and when they kick the shite
out of you in Fairview Park,
That's alright baby that's alright.

Dance with me
hold me closer
and when the morning comes
up the bright white steps
we'll go and find some other
twilight shadows dropping slow
and then we might ... then we might.
Run!
Run for your fucking life!
The boots ... the boots
will kick it out of you.
Take those bloody high heels off
and run.
Hitch that skirt up fast
and put your trust
in panic-stricken flight,
No! Not in there
That's the park
and that is surely where
they'll do it to you,
They too need the darkness
of the night
in which to yell
Kick the shite
out of the steamers!

And out of you
and out of you
and out of you.
They do ...
they call you steamer
bent and gay
I did too
But now I say
I never knew.
Now I see
People you
and people you
and people you
And when the love looks in
and sees the love looking out,
And when the love looks out
and sees the love looking in
Maybe then
Maybe then
We can fucking well begin.

There Was a Crooked Man

I have never seen
a man as misshapen
as you before.
Bent over body
so bent over
that your face
is facing down,
the only thing you ever see
beneath you is the ground.
Who bent you over like that?
Have you ever seen the sky
or anything at all
that is up
while your face
is facing down?
You look like the weight
of what Jesus carried
is crushing you to the ground.
They could never crucify you
as you slow slow inch
around the town.
Your body is much too crooked
to nail up against the wood
and nobody ever could hope
to bury you without breaking bones
to straighten you out.
I wonder do you ever think
that you're beautiful
I do.
I wonder if anyone has

ever embraced you.
How do you embrace a man
whose crooked body
is crooked facing down?

The falling rain
is beating on your back.
Maybe it will wash away
the marks of what you carried
when your name was Simon
and the winding stony track
was made for two.
You
and somebody who
could straighten you up tomorrow
if he had a mind to.
Take up your cross daily
and follow me.
I don't think you have ever
had a chance to put it down
as you slow slow crooked inch
around the crooked town.

The Cure

'There ye are
great to see you
can I get you a jar?'

'Grand - a glass of orange please.'

'Are you jokin' me or what?
have a proper drink …
what'll it be - a small one?'

'An orange is all I want thanks.'

'You don't want a bloody orange.
A real drink - have a real one.'

'I don't want one thanks
An orange is grand.'

'Grand me arse - Jerry
give us two small ones.'

'No - that's not what I want at all.
Listen - I'll get it for myself.
Jerry … a glass of orange please.

'Oh - I see - that's how it is.
You're too bloody proud
to have a jar with me.
My drink isn't good enough for you
I know your fucking sort.'

'Listen - I tell you
what I'll do.
I'll have that jar with you

if you'll do one very simple thing.'

'What?'

'Answer this question
to my satisfaction.
Why is it so important to you
that I have that drink?'

'Important!! Important!!!
Listen pal - I couldn't give
a shite whether you have it or not.'

'That's grand so ... I'll have an orange please ...'

More Marion

When you told me
that you thought
you might be pregnant
I thought about
a third person
who would love look
like you
and I trembled too.
More Marion I thought
and more Marion is more
than I have ever dared
to hope.
There never was a more Marion
and now there is no Marion any more.

Do It Yourself

You'd swear that she knew
the men were watching
half-past five
in the cold November morning
and her getting dressed
slowly slowly slowly
curtains pulled back wide
window flooded light
and the other windows
across the road
dark in eye-staring
behind the curtain
furtive frenzy peeping
where bed-sit lonely men
crouched and watched
and celebrated their
black bleak desolation
with the single most
solitary ceremonial
known to solitary man.
When each of them
had done it
in single isolation
they went back to bed.
She went off to work
leaving her bedroom light
switched on for anybody
who wished to gaze
upon her white nightdress
limp, limp and limp across the back
of a hard chair.

Psychiatric Cliché Cure

A good kick up the arse is what you need.
Cop onto and get a grip on and shake yourself up.
Count your blessings.
I had twice your troubles when I was half your age
and never took an aspirin.
Think of people who've only got one foot
and no shoes and the one foot they've got
is in the grave.
You don't know when you're well off
That's half your trouble.

It's always darkest before the cloud
that has a tunnel in the silver lining.
A good dose of hardship is what you need.
Meals on a tray will never get you right.
When did you last say a prayer?
Get it out ... your best foot
Put it forward ... your finger.
The doctors can only do so much.
It's a bloody good rest you're having in here
So ford every mountain, climb every stream
with the power of positive whatdyemaycallit
and you'll never look back
which is what well and truly screwed up Lot's wife
and she never finished up in here.

Think the world owes you a living.
You wouldn't know a good day's work
if it upped and bit you.

God alone knows what your grandfather would say
if he saw you moping in here.
Him that was up at five every morning
walking the ten miles to work on a empty stomach
in a blizzard for two and six a week before tax.

You just can't beat it,
Rolling up the sleeves
putting your shoulder to the wall
your nose to the wheel
My God is that the time?
I can't stay in here all day listening to you.
Doesn't time fly when you're having a good chat
and remember - a trouble shared
is worth two in the grindstone
so think about what I've said to you
it's for your own good/bye!

For Rita With Love

You came home from school
on a special bus
full of people
who look like you
and love like you
and you met me
for the first time
and you loved me.
You love everybody
so much that it's not safe
to let you out alone.
Eleven years of love
and trust and time for you to learn
that you can't go on loving like this.
Unless you are stopped
you will embrace every person you see.
Normal people don't do that.
Some normal people will hurt you
very badly because you do.

Cripples don't look nice
but you embrace them.
You kissed a wino on the bus
and he broke down and cried
and he said 'Nobody has kissed me
for the last thirty years.
But you did.'
You touched my face
with your fingers and said
"I like you."

The world will never
be ready for you.
Your way is right
and the world will
never be ready.

We could learn everything
that we need to know
by watching you
going to your special school
in your special bus
full of people
who look like you
and love like you
and it's not safe
to let you out alone.
If you're not normal
there is very little hope
for the rest of us.

That Ireland Might Be Free

'Goodbye lovie,
We'll talk about it tonight.
A little brother for Sinead,
Aye ... or a sister ... it very well might,
It very well might be that.
We'll talk about it tonight,
And till tonight, I love you.'
Kiss.
Kiss.
Kiss.
And down the yard the car was parked
And just as well.
Key in the ignition
And a fireball out of hell
With bloody blast and blaze
And bits of brain are dripping
from the apple tree,
Left hand is hiding under next door's hedge
The right is fused around the key,
And all the bits they found are in a box,
That Ireland might be free.

Put That On Your Scales

I wish that someone
would ring me right now
and say - 'Hey - I love you, Pat
- I know all the parts
of you that you hate
and shame and hide away
and I love you, Pat.
I know you
In all of your secret places
and I love you.'

I never thought
that I could ever
feel as lonely
as this again.
I never did.
Or go through a whole day
without really laughing once
or twice I made a noise
that sounded like a laugh
but it wasn't.

I would love Jesus
to ring me now
and say - 'Hey - I love you, Pat
and I will never judge you
the way that you judge yourself.
I am your sister Brig
I am your best friend Don
I am the itinerant on

O'Connell Bridge,
Remember the one you
bought a burger and a coffee,
I am the prisoners in the jail,
the ones you filled with laughter,
I am your wheelchair friends
they love you, Pat
and so do bloody well I
so put that on your crazy scales
and judge it.'

I wish that someone
would ring me now
and say - 'Hey, Pat
- will you judge me?'
'cos right now I'd
forgive them everything
... Amen.

Cracks and Things

The man said to me
'That's not such a bad day
sure it's not?'
He was telling me
what it almost wasn't
and he was asking me
to affirm his non-statement.
So I screwed him up
by telling him
that it wasn't such a good day
either - sure it wasn't?

The woman asked me
'How are they all in Clontarf?'
I don't believe for one moment
that she could possibly want
all that detailed information
and even if she did,
how the fuck am I
supposed to know?

A man asked me
how she was cutting.

A woman asked me
how things were.

A man asked me
what the story was.

A woman asked me
how it was going.

A man asked me
how the crack was.

A woman asked me
if they were keeping me busy.

A doctor asked me
how are we today?
He wished to know whether
we were taking our tablets
to keep us well.

I think that in
a very oblique way
they were expressing
a vague interest in
how I was feeling.

So I told them
she was cutting
straight up the middle,
things were mighty,
the story was an omnibus edition,
the crack was ninety,
they had me run off my feet.
We were lashing the pills
down as fast as we could
get them out of the chemist's.

I think that I was actually
telling them how good I felt
but with all this talk about
things and cracks and stories
I can't really be sure.

It's not such a bad day though,
sure it's not?

You Have Never Seen Me

A very tall very thin girl
goes walking past my window every night,
I sit at my desk and watch her go
Very tall and very thin
and for an hour or so I write.
And then before I know it
She is returning home,
Very tall and very thin
and very much alone.

Last night she didn't come
and I missed her
and I didn't write,
maybe I'll knock on my window
and tell her that
when she comes again
on this or some other night.

Safety Net Wanted

I would love someone to say to me -
'Let go Pat - let it go and if you fall
I will surely catch you.'
I am tired of hitting the ground
and lying there until I pick myself up.

Holy God - you fell three times
and you picked yourself up again
but just look where it got you.
I wouldn't be wild about that myself.
Fair enough - you raised yourself up
from the dead with a bit of outside help
and a half a dozen angels.
If I came back after three days
my flat would be gone.

I would love someone to say to me -
'Let go Pat - let it go and if you fall
I will surely catch you.'
I'm not as heavy as I look,
honestly ...

For Dav With Love

I don't know how it feels
to be sentenced to life
imprisonment at birth,
locked into a futile body
and slumped into a chair
with wheels to carry you
from here to there to any
bloody where you want to go.
I don't know what it's like
not to be able to talk
or shout or roar at all
the parts of your body
which have never ever worked
nor ever will,
to be filled with all
the jagged frustration
of never being able to scream
at your arms and your legs
'Move! Go on damn you. Move!'
It must be sheer blasting hell
to have to listen to people
talking about you as if
you aren't even there
or as if you're some sort
of sub-normal being who lives
inside a chair with wheels.
You can't even tell them
to fuck off and take their
sugar condescension
someplace else.

It must be sheer blasting hell
to feel an ever-upwards surge
of towering creativity
poems such as no man or boy
has ever written before
poems which rant and roar
'Let us out!
For fuck's sake let us out!'
And you can only inch
by inch them onto paper
straddling your mother's thigh
and riding it as you would a horse
in front of the typewriter
and Holy God it's murder trying
to force your agonising body
forwards to indicate a key
and then Brighid strikes it.
Slow slow click click slow
out if clicking comes
as you drag yourself
up the hill to Calvary
leaving the words
streaking a bloody trail
of red behind you.
Jesus Christ made the journey only once
the way of the Cross is daily yours
and still you crooked grin.
What in the name of God
is going on inside
that anarchistic
troublemaking
boatrocking head of yours?

The only way we'll ever know
is what you choose to show us
through your poems.
The rest is secret
and the rest is silence
and the rest is locked in
where none of us will ever go
slow slow click click slow
up the hill to Calvary.

Seats Still Warm

Nothing is enough
The audience goes home.
Don't leave any cigarettes
burning in the dressing-room
and close the door behind you
as you go out into the street.
The silence of an empty theatre
when everybody has gone
can follow you for miles.
Don't go.
Please don't go.
I'll chop off my head for you
But how the fuck do you follow that?

Out Of Your Head

It felt good
every time you did it,
but the pleasure was bad
so you had to admit it
to a priest
on your knees
in the dark
so nobody sees
in a whisper
don't say it out loud
waiting their turn
there's a hell of a crowd
mustn't let them
hear your shame
although
three of the times
you weren't to blame
three of the times
it happened in your sleep
sex is alright
so long as you keep
your hands to yourself
and you're not awake
you'll only burn
for the chances you take
when the feeling is good
but the pleasure is bad
and you know what you're doing
from instruction you've had
grave matter

full consent
kneel in the dark
kneel and repent
forbidden thoughts
how many times?
eighty seven
but to lessen my crimes
I only enjoyed
sixty percent
forbidden flickers
to heaven I went
but now you're off
to hell and back
soul scorched
blacker than black
grinding guilt
is making you pay
crushing you dizzy
making you say
I didn't mean it
never again
I'll be good
for ever amen
thrilling thoughts
out of your mind
hands to yourself
get thee behind
head bent
fear of hell
keep a count
of the times you fell
make a list

tot up the score
heavenly peace
body at war
saw nakedness
strayed from the path
not so bad
was yourself in the bath
that's allowed
offence there is none
providing you didn't turn yourself on
out of your head
out of your mind
buy yourself handcuffs
before you go blind
if it's good
it's bad
if it's pleasure there's sin
grace is the state
your head is done in
numb your body
freeze your mind
kill the flickers
get thee behind
deny the senses
strict control
cold showers
good as gold
kill the feelings
kill them dead
out of your mind
and out of your head …

Some Girls Prefer

Some girls prefer to undress in the dark,
"Do you mind if I turn out the light?
Later you can touch me and kiss me and hold
but don't look,
it doesn't feel right."
Some girls prefer to undress in the dark,
"Would you mind also closing your eyes?
Later you can fondle and feel and caress
but you're forbidden to look at the prize."

Shy with my body
a prisoner of clothes
naked is hidden away
under the covers
where nobody knows
the words I prefer not to say,
words for the parts
I sometimes disown,
my nose and my ears are alright,
but some other bits
belong in the dark
they belong in the shadows of night.

I'll call it my pussy
that doesn't sound wrong
pussy sounds cosy and nice
nothing could be finer
but don't mention vagina
you're hinting at naughties and vice.
Pussy and willy,

willy sounds good
willy is as good as gold,
but Lord between us
don't mention a penis
unless you're a doctor
it's bold.

Go to the mirror
and take a good look
at your body
there's no need for shame.
Your body is beautiful
and not just in parts
each segment has got its own name.
So hello to you arm
how's it goin' there leg?
examine your body with pride,
what's the story, left ear?
how's she cuttin' there, nose?
discover you've got nothing to hide.
More power to you penis
you're a part of me too
and vagina, you're welcome aboard,
when your body is whole
and you own all your parts
the parts you've so often ignored.
That's getting it together
that's feeling as one
a feeling that's healthily right,
a glorious buzz
whole and entire
and now YOU CAN TURN ON THE LIGHT!

Tinker's Biddies

Marie's arms and legs don't work
and she laughs a lot.
Spasm sort of twitches
which never move the way
she wants them to.
The only noise she makes
sounds like 'Yes'
and unless you're very careful
she'll playful nip your fingers
with her teeth when you're
feeding her at teatime.
Tea gurgle slurp swallow dribbles
and when you say, 'You tinker's biddy'
she nearly chokes herself
with the laughing.
She tells you with her eyes
that she hates lettuce
and twitches with excitement
when she sees you coming.
Looking, staring, willing
you to see the bag of crisps
on the bed and even though
she's gallon full of tea
happily you stuff her mouth
with crisps and happily
she eats them.
Suddenly little Caroline is helping too
wheelchair parked beside Marie's
dipping chubby four years fingers
into the bag of crisps

and making her own little noises
which sound unlike any words
you've ever heard
or ever will
Easing shaky crisps into Marie's mouth
safe as houses with her fingers
for Marie is being tender careful
with her teeth.
Eleven years of spasm twitches
is grinning at the sight
of tangle curled Caroline
eating every second crisp herself.
A right pair of tinker's biddies
if ever I saw one
looking at each other
and love laugh loving
who they see.
Tinker's biddies
please love laugh look
at me.

Tonight They Put the Cotsides Up

Tonight they put the cotsides up
onto the old man's bed,
'You can't fall out and hurt yourself'
that's what the nurses said.
And God you should have seen it,
you should have seen his face,
as metal sides both rattled
and bolts clanked into place.

He sat there numb
and silent
silent
and very very still,
and nobody who saw him,
nobody every will
forget the way the colour
drained right out of his face,
as metal sides both rattled
and bolts clanked into place.

The nurses said the cotsides
were to keep him safe in bed,
'You can't fall out and hurt yourself'
that's what the nurses said.
The rest of us lay looking,
we knew that no matter how far
that old man fell in future
it could never leave a scar
the way those cotsides did.

Nobody wanted to catch his eye,
he was curled up silent and still,
maybe he'll go asleep for us,
that's it - maybe he will
go asleep embraced in a cradle,
in the morning they'll take
the sides down,
Go asleep embraced in a cradle
that's the way Jesus was found.

You couldn't go over and talk to him
for that would only mean ...
you couldn't go over and talk to him
for then you'd have to lean
and look in over the top,
nobody wanted to do that,
remind him of the way you'd stop
and gaze at a new born infant.
And merciful God you couldn't peep,
peeping through the bars would be worse,
You couldn't go over and talk to him,
softly he started to curse,
'Do yez think I'm a bloody baby,
Do yez think I'm a baby or what?'
then he sank down under the covers,
in between the sides of his cot.

Tonight they put the cotsides up,
onto the old man's bed,
'You can't fall out and hurt yourself'
that's what the nurses said.
The rest of us lay looking

we knew that no matter how far
that old man fell in future
it could never leave a scar
the way those cotsides did.

My Inaccessible Poem For Everybody Who Needs One

Irridescent voluminous fear
trembling amid momentous
callibrating essence
of nebulised nettleweed.
Yet heady pallor
when you left
with knuckle cracking knock
on non-existent kneecaps.
Yet in spite of all this
Uncle Edgar is still eating
sardine sandwiches
with phosphorescent sergeant-majors
and living alone in a beeloud glade
leads inexorably into neolythic
emasculated marginally melted
liquorish pipes are all in a row.

No - You Ask Him

A million people know his face,
'There he is ... look ... that's him.'
'It is.'
'It isn't.'
'It is.'
'It isn't.'
'Ask him.'
'No - you ask him.'
'Excuse me - are you your man?'
On the bus and in the train,
'Ask him'
'No - you ask him.'
Ask him dizzy
ask him again and again and again,
in the shops and on the street
and in a million places where some
of the million people meet.
Drinking a coffee,
Having a pee,
'Quick ... quick ... look look,
No - not one autograph,
I want three,
For Kevin and Samantha and Jane.'
'It is ... it isn't.'
'It is ... it isn't.'
Dizzy and dizzy
Dizzy and dizzy again,
'Twenty Silk Cut please.'
Hey - aren't you Your Man?
Hey you

Hey you
Hey you
Sign this this and this
Yeah - I know you're doing a piss
but I'm in a hurry.
Hey you
You're great
You're thick
Tell us a joke
Do us a trick.
It's well for you
You've got it made
Your money comes easy
Come out of the shadows
Come out of the shade,
Samantha wants to see you,
God - you're not like you at all
You look tired
What about all the crack
What about the times
you made us laugh?
Here - sign this,
No - I don't want the one,
I want a million,
For Jason and Marion and Natalie and Mark and Darren
    and Simon and Mandy and Jennifer and Susie and
    Gerry and Vince and Anto and Sarah and ...

Boxer in a Bottle

Dribbling drooling drunk
broken nose booze battered
boxer reeling
and remembering thirty years back
when the gloves were raised
and the crowd was roared
and the celebration drinks
were copeable
and didn't leave you
dribbling drooling drunk
and empty eyed asking
'Where did it get me?
Won forty fights
and where did it get me?'
Sunburned and booze blitzed
in the Galway street
with no ropes to hang onto
and no hope of ever winning
the fight you don't even
realise is on.
'I can't seem to get drunk anymore.'
That's what you said.
'I can't seem to get drunk anymore.'
If you fell you'd miss the ground.
If this is not the last round
it's because the barman is calling
'Time now ladies and gentlemen please,'
Time to fuck you back out onto the street,
'I can't seem to get drunk anymore.'
It is not humanly possible to get any drunker.

Nobody counts you out anymore
They fuck you out instead
and whatever is inside your head
is fired out with you.
The road is narrowing to a point
somewhere not too far on front
and it's going right through you
for a short cut.
Put your hands up over your head
and listen.
The crowd stopped roaring thirty years ago
and they're not coming back.
Maybe you can hear the roar
and that's why you keep on trying.
Boxer in a bottle
is dribbling drooling drunk
... and dying ...

Penis Poem

There are twelve penises in a dozen
but it is highly unlikely
that anybody in Ireland
will ever tell you that.

I Know My Telegraph Poles

I cannot imagine the terrible things
that railway telegraph poles do
when they are free.
The only ones I ever see
are being forcibly restrained
all along the embankment
at the side of the tracks.
Forcibly restrained
and anchored down by cables
so they won't all hunt in packs.
Would they chase sheep
from Kildare to main-line stations or what?
Would they creep up behind railway workmen
and boot them into tunnels?
I know that I have got
no need to worry
if they ever slip their chains.
I know that my card will be safely marked
when they lie across the tracks
to stop the trains
and put the heart across the people
who never raised a finger
that the captives might be free.
I know my telegraph poles
and my telegraph poles know me.
"That's Pat" they'll say,
"Don't boot Pat - he's O.K.
He founded the Telegraph Pole
Liberation front ... no - don't hunt him.
Even now he's got a wire cutters
shoved up underneath his jumper."

And then I'll lead them one by one
Into a verdant valley
where restraining cables will be none
and telegraph poles will skip
and jump and dance and run
around in whooping circles
and ever will be free.
I know my telegraph poles
and my telegraph poles know me.

A Thought For The Day

Who first discovered
how to milk a cow
and what in the name of God
were they trying to do
at the time?

For Don

There is no place to hide
When you stand up on the stage
and say 'Good evening everyone,
You're very welcome.'
Nobody knows how you're feeling,
They didn't see you in your dressing room,
but they sure as hell can see you now.
I listen to the notes you blow
and I hear the secret beating of your soul,
You're holding nothing back Don
And anybody who has got ears to hear
can hear it.
Out comes the past and the present
and the hope and the fear and the pain,
I know how much it takes for you
to take up that harp
on the nights when your body
is screaming at you
to take up something else
and you take up your harp
and anybody who has got ears to hear
can hear it.
Out comes the long roads
and the desolation
of a million empty railway stations.
And suddenly you're celebrating
and blowing out with love and guts
and sheer bloody genius.
A man in a million
and I'm proud that you're my friend.

Up there on top is where you belong
and I'm getting a powerful buzz
watching you getting there.
You're holding nothing back
and anybody who has got ears to hear
can hear it.
I can.

Now I Have You!

'I bet you don't remember me.'
Triumphant grinning face
shoved up nose to nose to mine.
I've learned how to defuse
this one the hard way.
Politely at first ...
'You are quite right
I can't place you.
Tell me where we met
and then perhaps I might.'
But he wants to play the game
refuses to be defused.
'God but you're a nice one.
You mean to say ... you've forgotten!
Like ... you honestly don't remember.'

I'll defuse this bastard
if it kills he, she, me or it.
'Listen man - I only ever remember
people who make an impression.
You wouldn't make one
if you plunged down 10,000 feet
into wet concrete.
In fact right now
you are in the running
for the proud title
ONE OF THE TRULY GREAT FORGETTABLE
FACES OF OUR TIME.'
'But you must know me
you must remember.

I shook hands with you in Wexford
the summer before last.'
'Why didn't you say that?!!
You should have told me.
Now I have you.
Now it all comes flooding back.
You shook hands with me
and you said ... don't tell me
you said ... 'I bet you don't
remember me' ...

The Ultimate Self-pity Poem

Everyone else is better than me and I'm no good
at anything. There's no point in trying because
I'll only fail.
MOAN.
I'm not going to talk to anyone because I
can't think of anything to say. Besides, other
people's silences are much more articulate
than mine.
MOAN AND SIGH.
I'm completely finished and it's all downhill
from now on. My hill on which it's all down
isn't nearly as steep as other people's.
MOAN SIGN AND MOAN AGAIN.
Other people are spectacular failures. I'm
only a very ordinary one. I wallow in self pity.
Other people drown magnificently in theirs.
SOB AND TREMBLE.
My psychiatrist doesn't understand the grave
nature of my disturbances. He goes away for
five weeks' holidays and doesn't give me the
number of his hotel.
LOOK TRAGIC.
If anyone else wrote this poem, everybody
would say - 'Isn't it great.' But because I
wrote it, they're saying - 'He even makes a balls out of
    being negative.'
COLLAPSE.

Unofficial Sin

They've got a word for it.
Supposing that you say
'I'll never get anywhere
near an eternal reward.
Heaven hath no place
for the randy such as me.'
One ... two ... three ...
You've just done it.
That's Despair
and that's a sin.

Supposing that you say
'I'm as good as there,
Me and God groovin' together
forever and ever,
We've got it made,
God and me.'
One ... two ... three ...
You've just done it.
That's Presumption
and that's a sin.

But what about a bit of both?
What about maybe I will
and maybe I won't?
'Cos sometimes I do
and sometimes I don't.
Presumption and Despair,
A little bit you, a little bit me.
One ... two ... three ...

You've just done it.
That's Desbumption
but that's not a sin
... yet.
So go to it,
Commit it while it's unofficial
and stocks last.
Congratulations my son
on a truly imaginative sin,
Congratulations my son
and come on in ...

Warning

A grasshopper looked
at himself in a mirror
through a magnifying glass
and gave himself
a cardiac arrest.
If you have to look
at yourself in a mirror
through something,
the reducing end
of a telescope
is best.

Please Notice Me

Please look over
and notice me,
See - I'm standing here
with a drink in my hand
pretending to be
utterly unconcerned,
Leaning against the wall
and doing my very best
to look as if I haven't
noticed you at all,
Please look over
and catch my eye
and smile.
It's bloody hard work
standing here
trying to appear
fascinating and handsome
in a mysterious brooding
enigmatic way,
Please smile and walk over
and say "Hey - I really would
like to talk to you ...
You're the man who grooves
through the most indescribable
fantasies I have ever had
Ooooh - I'm so glad
that you have chosen me
to ignore."
Please look over
and implore me

with your eyes
I'm working my arse off
standing here trying
to disguise the fact
that I would love
to talk to you.
But there's nothing I can do
until someone makes the first move
and that will have to be you.
I'm much too busy
trying to think of a million
devastating things to say
to make you want to know me
for my body and my mind
and any other bits of me
which you may find interesting.

No, No - ignore that guy
the one who's posing and shaping
and smiling at you.
I know his sort
he'll try to whip
the drawers off you
before he even knows your name
I know his game
You'll be much better off with me
I lost my virginity
by accident when I was 23
and I haven't found it since.

Please look over and notice me
this place will be closing soon

and you and I will finish our drinks
and never ever know
I don't want to go home by myself
is how I always seem to be
so please look over
  please look over
    and notice me.

I Have Never Seen ...

I have never seen ...
  a bus driver wearing a seat belt.
  a steamroller with an 'L' plate.
  a wheelchair person working in RTE, a department
    store (add to this list yourself).
  two elephants making love.
  an adult enjoying a good laugh in a church.
  a bank manager playing a banjo.
  a girl in a mini-skirt who doesn't look daggers at you
    if you admire her legs.
  any man I loved as much as my father.
  a queue at the GPO which moves slower
    than the one I'm in.
  the secret place where all my combs
    and nailfiles hide.
  a bishop on a bus.
  Nellie's room behind the wallpaper.
  a millibar rising or falling slowly.
  safety engineers stress testing O'Connell Bridge.
  the place from which the twelve mile
    fisheries limit starts.
  an itinerant using a PASS machine.
  a T.D. in my flat.
  a woman driving a train.
  as many tri-colours flying proudly at full mast as we
    see at half-mast when somebody famous
    and Irish has died.
  Fidel Castro.

Claddagh Young Man

Red-haired brown-freckled
growing up very young man
from the Claddagh.
Casting your fishing line
out and over black water.
Over there the Spanish
landed wine and port
and your grandfather
looks out from a brown
and yellow faded photograph
of the brown and yellow
faded men from the Claddagh.
You look out towards
the Spanish Arch
and splash your line
into the black and Spanish water.
You know that the boat beneath you
is old two hundred years
and the water all around you
is as old as you want it to be.
You know things about the ropes
and the wind and the salt
that nobody ever Claddagh told you
and that's how old you are.

Ring-a-ring-a-rosy

Forty-seven thousand ants
marched two by two
into my inner ear
while I was sleeping
and now they're playing
ring-a-ring-a-rosy
and seriously upsetting
my sense of balance.
I am only able to walk
without falling down
when they are all sound
asleep.
The mathematical chances
of forty-seven thousand ants
all being asleep at the same time
are so bloody slim
that now I'm forced to spend
most of my waking hours within
a no-gravity simulation chamber
where the ring-a-ring-a-rosy
of the forty-seven thousand ants
jerks me up and down
and whirls me round and round
so in a sense I sort of
ring-a-ring-a-rosy too
There's really not much else
that I can do.

Rock On, Little Bee

The train from Galway to Dublin
stopped in the middle of nowhere
so that I was able to watch a bee
working his little arse off
at ten past eight at night,
buzzing and blossom-blitzing
in a wild hedgerow
beside the railway.
Little bee - I'm thrilled that
I caught a glimpse of you and
I hope that they bloody well
appreciate you back at the hive.
Your honey is worth bottling.
Then the train took off again
and left you somewhere that was
in the middle of nowhere to me
but was the centre of your universe.
Rock on, little bee,
I've decided to keep on rockin' too
since I caught a centre of the universe
glimpse of you.

Suicide ... The Irish Cure

Fear of Hell
keeps you in this one.

For Hughie

Your drumkit is silent now, Hughie,
your sticks lie still on the floor,
I won't see you riding your bockedy bike,
or warm to your Hughie smile any more.
Away from the drums you were quiet and shy,
and meeting you was always truly good
we talked about music and we talked about bands,
and we laughed like men with golden earrings should.
We stood beside your bockedy car
and we listened to each other's crazy dreams
you too gentle for a game without rules
a business that's not always what it seems.
You got some really rough breaks
I never once heard you complain,
you're the bravest person I have ever known,
courage and dignity through pain.
I'm proud to have known you,
I'm proud that we met,
I wouldn't have had it any other way,
I wish you love and peace and rest,
Hughie ... I salute you today.

Out Of Mind

You can't see in
the walls are high
bus full of people
speeding by
safe distance
lock and key
fleeting glimpse
home for tea
out of sight
out of mind
thanks be to God
they're safe behind
high walls
locked doors
their own fault
not mine or yours
life goes on
they don't exist
forgotten men
department list
shut them in
lock them out
soundproof walls
in case they shout
what's it like?
We haven't a clue
it needn't bother
me or you.
Does it work?
Why ask me?

I've things to do
people to see
not my problem
I'm in the clear
I pay my taxes
every year,
their own fault
I fail to see
why can't they live
like you and me?
A clear choice
black or white
lock them up
serves them right
time to think
learn new ways
social conscience
one of these days
we'll let them out
sentence is done
holy shit
they're on the run
a week of freedom
they'll never learn
back inside
another turn
waste of time
love in vain
turn the key
lock them up
again ...

It's Not So Bloody Funny

She laughs at everything
that he says
and he laughs at everything
that she says.
He wants to take her
back to his place.
She wants a lift home
to save the taxi fare.
So she laughs at everything
that he says
and he laughs at everything
that she says.
Now he's laughing
and touching her
and she's laughing
and touching him
and he's saying
my car is outside
and she's saying
I'd never have guessed
and he's saying
my place for a coffee
and she's saying
it's very late
and he's saying
I'll drop you
straight home
afterwards
and she's saying
I've got work

in the morning
and he's saying
ten minutes then
and she's saying
not tonight Nigel
and he's not laughing
and she's not laughing
and she's going
back to her friend
and he's wearing his
it doesn't matter
to me face
and ten minutes later
he's laughing at everything
that somebody else says
and she's laughing at everything
that somebody else says
and you don't really
have very much choice.
Otherwise you'd cry
your bloody eyes out.

We're O.K.

I asked you to sort out
the mug full of pens
on my desk
and dump all the ones
that had gone dry.
And now I have another
reason why I love you.
Next day I found them
hidden away.
All the useless pens
you couldn't bring
yourself to dump
and I loved you
like I've never
loved before
because I do exactly
the same and more
when I'm helping
on my friend's trawler,
throwing live crabs
back into the sea
when nobody is looking.
We're a right pair
you and me.
Pens and crabs
have nothing to fear
and as long as
both of us
keep on doing
those lovely crazy things
neither have we.

Don't Wake The Daisies

I have never loved
you so much as
when you looked at
the tightly closed bud
on the flowers
in the vase
on the table
in the restaurant
and your eyes moistened.
'That would have been
a flower,' you said.

I have never loved
you so much as
when we walked
on the grass
at two in the morning
and you pointed
at the daisies
with their petals
folded up for the night.
'Look - they're asleep,'
you whispered
as if you were afraid
you would waken them up.

I have never loved
you so much as
when we sat
on the floor

in my flat
and watched the sky
orange red and green
explode with fireworks
and you looked at
the crowds as well
and softly said
'I wonder how many
of those people
will go down to
Dollymount beach
in the morning
to watch the sunrise.'

Now I look at clouds again.
Now I notice the shapes
of shadows.
Now I look at my nose
in the mirror.
I wish that I could
look at me and see
who you see.
Until I figure out
a way to do that
I'll just have to
take your word for it.

A Fearful Pee

Feeling fear
full of fear
oh Jesus I'm afraid.
But nobody knows
to look at me.
Nobody has got a clue
not even you
who loves me.
Years of going up on a stage
and letting the punters see me
easy, laid-back, laughing, cool,
who the hell is fooling who?
What?!
Whistle a happy tune?
Don't be so bloody ridiculous ...
The only one I know is
How Can You Solve A Problem Like Maria
and it's not her I'm worried about.
So I'm going out
out of my flat and down to the sea,
I'm going to splash a lovely
arching rainbow spiral pee
into the water
and think about all the people
who are swimming on the other side,
if the tide is in the right direction
they'll be swimming in my wee wee
and they won't even know it.
They won't have a clue,
now even you,
who loves me.